Reflections

Inspirational Thoughts

To Live

Your Best Life

CJ Marie

To my family and friends
who are the jewels in my life.
Know how much you are appreciated and loved.

Books by C.J. Marie

Reflections
Words of Wisdom
Accents of a Women
Captured Thoughts
Afterthoughts of Yesterday
Legacy of Stable Dreams
Shadowed Love
Reflections of Time
Melody of Love
Days of Difference
Echoes from the Heart

Children's Stories:
Mi Primer Dia-Escolar
My First Day in Kindergarten

Chap Books:
Of Love and Sorrow
Fly With Your Dreams

Guides:
Tell Me What to Do
Pageant Tips

Acknowledgements

It is with great appreciation to
Joe, Matthew, and Rocco
for all their help in assisting me to complete this book.

Contents

The Power of Words: A Foreword

C.J. Marie is my grandmother, who I call, "Nana." Through the years my Nana has been a powerful influence on me. Every time I pick up one of Nana's books I learn something. Many times through her writings I get to understand and furthermore, appreciate the Power of Words. In Nana's most recent book, Reflections, it is clear to see and understand what I mean.

There are many words in the English language and so many of them are powerful. Therefore, when combining words into phrases and quotes there can be so much more inspiration, motivation, and knowledge learned. That is the **Power of Words**.

What you will come to find in the coming pages are the power-filled quotes, C.J. Marie has either collected from various sources or created them for herself. In between the quotes, you will also read essays, these essays are thoughts furthering the quotes or ideas. Every single expression will leave your mind pondering and recognizing the truth, authenticity, and sincerity in each one of these ideas. C.J. Marie has done a fantastic job compiling and building on the true definition of the **Power of Words**.

Matthew Mazza
March 2023

Introduction

As I began gathering quotes for this book, I realized how much I was learning about myself. Each of these quotes, reflect on similar themes throughout the book. These themes include optimism, hope, understanding, awareness, and gratitude. They echo all that is important in life. As you read these, some will resonate with you and your life. That means there is a thread of truth about yourself in that writing. If you apply it to your life and really give it thought, you could identify how you are living your own life presently.

Allowing yourself to be in touch with your inner self, you can see and question the direction your life has taken. Did you have a dream? Are you a grateful person? Do you love life? Are you an optimistic individual or a pessimist at heart? Only you can answer these questions. My objectives in these collections of writings are for you to get in touch with your inner self. It's never a waste of time to know more about who you are.

It gives you an opportunity to stop and re-evaluate your way of thinking. Ask yourself what makes me think that way? These thoughts give way to new ideas. Ideas that can be described as dreams, and dreams are vital in life. Most of us don't think in terms of the importance of dreams, but your plans in life are dreams you hope to accomplish. I see dreams as aspirations that drive us to achieve them. My essays are thoughts I live by today that I have arrived at from writing my personal quotes.

My hope is that you will find peace and self-recognition as you contemplate these words. They have the potential to be life changing, however you must be able to look at yourself honestly and live the life you choose in your own unique way.

When we come with a lot of baggage the
trip becomes very interesting.

— C.J. Marie

Enjoy the little things in life
With one hand we try to press forward
And the other hand holds us back.

—C. J Marie

What years take away, wisdom,
Insight, and knowledge is given back.

I acted as if what you said meant nothing
But it broke my heart.

— C.J. Marie

A fact about life is that we will age, we will die
But what really counts is what we make from the journey.
Champion the truth you live by.

— C.J.Marie

◆

Experience is priceless
You pay for it with your youth.

◆

Peace can only come from forgiveness.

◆

Fan the flames of anger forgive and move on.

◆

I am a perfect imperfection
With extraordinary magic striving
For perfection in an ordinary life.

— C.J. Marie

◆

*Live your life
Instead of obsessing about it.*

— C.J. Marie

*A master communicator
is a master connector.*

— C.J. Marie

*Freedom comes from letting go of people and things
That give us pain, live the life your worthy of living
In this world.*

— C.J. Marie

We make a life by what we give

— Winston Churchill

There is a difference between a vision and a mission
A vision is what we would like to happen
A mission is ways we make it happen.

Remember to live out loud.

– C.J. Marie

◆

My memories are treasures that live
In my heart.

– C.J. Marie

◆

Be Connected to Yourself

What does it mean to be connected? The definition is to be attached, joined together, relate, link, unite, combine. There are many words related to being "connected". To be connected to ourselves means to tune into your thoughts and know who you are. There is no relationship more important than the one you have with yourself.

It takes time to look within and understand what really makes us who we are. Bear in mind there are many facets and dimensions that make us who we are. Many times, we view ourselves as the underdogs. There are emotions, sensations impulses, and thoughts that stimulate us. We must be aware of our strengths and weaknesses.

All these factors are the foundation of the decisions we make. Express your feelings, and always be mindful of your thoughts and emotions. Listen and be appreciative of yourself. Distractions prevent us from turning into ourselves and taking notice. Being aware is the gateway to self-improvement, self-knowledge, and direction to a more peaceful and happy life.

You have to live it to understand it.

— C.J.Marie

Winners never quit
And quitters never win.

Lies spread quicker than the truth
Beware!

— C.J. Marie

Life's tragedy is that we get old too soon
And wise too late.

— Benjamin Franklin

Ask yourself is it better to live with guilt or regret?

— C.J. Marie

When your young your whole life is about the pursuit of fun.
Then you grow up and learn to be cautious,
You can break a home or a heart.
You look before you leap and sometimes you don't leap at all
Because there may not be someone to catch you.
In life there is no safety net.
When did it stop being fun and start being scary?

How can a mother cut her child out of her life
Isn't a mothers love unconditional?

We make the best decisions based on what we know.

– C.J.Marie

Vintage women are aged to perfection.

– C.J. Marie

Don't loose youself trying to please others
Even if you loose everyone, you have
Found yourself and that is priceless.

– C.J. Marie

If you believe you could you will.

Don't underestimate me I know more than I say
I think more than I speak, and notice more than you realize.

– From *The Power of Positivity*

Learn to embrace your imperfections its those unique
Differences that make you extraordinary.

Celebrate your age, so many never make it.

– C.J. Marie

The only lasting beauty is the beauty of the heart.

— Rumi

You have to be unique and different and
Shine your own way.

— Lady Gaga

Failure is another stepping stone to greatness.

— Oprah Winfrey

Senior women demonstrate senior excellence.

— C.J. Marie

The 3 most important factors to make a dream come true
Are vision, perserverance and determination.

— C.J. Marie

Being authentic, genuine and unique
means you're not plastic or fake.
Make certain they know you're the real deal.

– C.J. Marie

◆

Never give up, never back down, and never stop dreaming.

– President Donald Trump

◆

If you really want something you will find a way
If you don't you will find an excuse.

◆

Youth is wasted on the young.

– Bernard Shaw

◆

The best thing you can give the world
Is the best version of yourself.

◆

A woman is like a tea bag, until you put it
In hot water do you know how strong she is.

– Eleanor Roosevelt

Flashbacks

A return to the past, a place where I have been happy and felt safe, surrounded by the love of my grandparents. The past is a difficult place, however the mind seems to retrieve the memories from time to time.

When I think of times long-ago, the memories are ever so clear. I can walk through the rooms I grew up in and remember every detail. It is almost like being hypnotized and reliving the steps of my youth. Sometimes in the midst of my memories it feels like I'm in a trance and I need to quickly distract myself before it overtakes me. It is ironic to me that as life unfolds when many decades have passed, those memories come to the forefront of our minds and we realize how precious those times were. The birthdays, the holidays and the special occasions being surrounded by all our loved ones, and we now see how everything has changed. Our loved ones have passed away and our relatives have moved far away. Sometimes, it's difficult to keep a good perspective.

If we could only go back to those days just for a short time and relive those times and be with those we love one more time. Reality strikes and we need to focus on the present, leaving those treasured memories behind and being grateful for the blessings we have now. The power of our thoughts is very strong. It can engulf us and stir up feelings both good and bad. Putting all of this in perspective takes a conscious effort. We can't live in the past. We can respect it, enjoy the bittersweet memories and if we are smart, know when to move on and not get caught up in the web of what was.

Its good to look back at the past
As long as you don't stare at it.

Lets transform winter dreams into summer magic.

Me and you
Just us two.

– From a *Sex in the City* episode

Grow old with me, the best is yet to come.

Train longer finish stronger.

Its amazing what we do to live out our dreams.

Time waits for no one it passes you by
It goes on forever like clouds in the sky.

— Giocchina Jennie Villareale

Everyone you know is fighting a battle
you know nothing about
Be kind.

Life is in the moment don't worry about the future.
A friend is a another self.

— Aristotle

Its good to have champagne wishes and cavier dreams.

— C.J. Marie

Maybe our mistakes are what makes our fate.
Without them what would shape our lives?
Perhaps if we never veered off course we wouldn't fall in love,
or have babies or be who we are.
After all seasons change. So do cities.
People come into our life and people go.
But its comforting to know that the ones you love
are always in your heart,
and if you're very lucky only a plane ride away.

– Carrie Bradshaw, *Sex and the City*

◆

There comes a time in every relationship
When romance gives way to reality.

◆

You can never go back to the way
Life used to be, time moves on and
So should you

– C.J. Marie

◆

The most important thing in life is your family.
There are days you love them, and others you don't.
But in the end they are the people you always come home to.
Sometimes it's the family your born into
and sometimes it's the one you make for yourself.

◆

Never be a prisoner of your past.

◆

Die young as old as possible.

– George H. W. Bush

◆

The difference between winning and losing is detail.

◆

Attitude is ageless
Its like an injection of youth.

◆

A life without purpose is a life without meaning.

– Rick Warren

The bond between a mother and a son is a special one.
It remains unchanged by time or distance.

The heart will always hold what the mind no longer can.

Its easier to be forgiven than to ask for permission.

Believe in the beauty of your dreams.

Don't try to fit in
You were born to stand out.

Listen with your mind but
Always follow your heart.

Maybe the past is like an anchor
Holding us back.
Maybe you have to let go of who you were
To become who you will be.

— Carrie Bradshaw, *Sex and the City*

They say nothing lasts forever,
Dreams change, trends come and go
But friendship never goes out of style.

— Carrie Bradshaw, *Sex and the City*

Its not about who's real to your face.
It's about who stays loyal behind your back.

— Marilyn Monroe

Some people come into our lives as blessings
Some come in your life as lessons.

– Danielle Steel

Elegance is the only beauty
That never fades

– Audrey Hepburn

To the world you may be one person
But to one person you are the world.

– Bill Wilson

There's nothing more beautiful
than the way the ocean refuses
To stop kissing the shoreline,
no matter how many times its sent away.

–Sarah Kay

There are many reasons to feel good about you.
There are obstacles you've overcome
and the challenges you've met.
There's the wisdom you've gained
and the progress you've made.
There are the lives you've touched
and the wonderful qualities that make you
an incredible person.

You are whimisical, vibrant, statement making,
You stand out in a crowd. You are pulled together well.
You value your own strength and follow your own lead.
You are comfortable in your own skin
and confident in your own life.
You totally live life your way.

If your afraid of conflict to keep the peace
You start a war inside yourself.

— Cheryl Richardson

A hero is someone who has given his or her life
To something bigger than oneself.

– Joseph Campbell

◆

Pretty is an accident of nature
Elegant is a self created work of art.

–Bing Caballero

◆

Live In the Moment

We all think we have time. So many of us take time for granted. Unless our attention is brought to the precious moments of time, as we live each day, we do not recognize them. It is brought to the forefront when health is in question or tragedy arises. Time is elusive, it passes quickly without realizing it.

So, the motto to live by is, "Live your Life", this is not a dress rehearsal, heed each moment. Feel it, absorb it, and be conscious of it. There are many beautiful blessings surrounding us, feel life, and there is no time to waste. Unfortunately, sometimes we are too busy to stop and give gratitude. Tomorrow is promised to no one.

Bad days make you appreciate
The good ones.

When the power of love
Overcomes the love of power
The world will know peace.

Age is just a number and numbers
Have no power over you,
Unless you allow them to.
Its all a numbers game, invented
To frighten you.

Sometimes the most simplest moment
Becomes the most treasured memory.

If you want the rainbow
You have to put up with the rain.

Memories are treasures of the heart
Always to be remembered.

– C.J. Marie

Photos are memories without words
frozen in time.

– C.J. Marie

Life has more imagination
Than we carry in our dreams.

Its always better to marry someone
who loves you more than
You love them.

Failures are preparations for victories.

Time stood still
as we sorted through
a graveyard of memories.

– Dr. David Mazza

I choose to live by my choice
Not by chance
To make changes not excuses
To be motivated not manipulated
To be useful
Not used
To excel
Not to compete
I choose self esteem
Not self pity
I choose to listen to
My inner voice,
Not the random opinion of others.

Weak people seek revenge
Strong people forgive
Intelligent people ignore.

– Albert Einstein

I will not apologize for being me.

The beauty in life is simply seen
When you take the time
to open your eyes to see it.

– C.J. Marie

Own every step you take
Believe in yourself
Walk with confidence
Know who you are
It doesn't matter what anyone thinks.

– C.J. Marie

Celebrate, elevate, and recognize
safe space without judgement.

◆

Gratitude knows no bounds.

◆

Never take criticism from anyone
Who you wouldn't take advice from.

◆

Possibilities

There are times in our life when we limit ourselves to the prospects of opportunity. Often fear stands in our way of challenge. Pessimistic and negative outcomes fill our mind and prevent us from exploring what could be beneficial to us. As individuals we grow when we go beyond our comfort zone, to the unknown. We learn and conquer, in hopes of bettering ourselves with knowledge. It takes courage to face the unknown, opportunities come and go and if we don't take a chance on them, they may be gone forever. The should've, could've thoughts enter our minds and regret will set in. I have always found it beneficial to set my fear aside and take on a new challenge.

You never know what you can do until you are tested. It can unveil new possibilities in your life. We should proceed and leave no stone unturned in our lives. You never know how strong you are until you face your fear and triumph over it.

Can you ever really forgive
If you can't forget?

In a field of roses she is a wildflower.

The most exciting challenging and significant
relationship of all is the one you have with yourself.

— Carrie Bradshaw, *Sex and the City*

You have to love yourself first
Before you can really love anyone else.

— C.J. Marie

Maybe some women were
Never meant to be tamed.

— Carrie Bradshaw, *Sex and the City*

It's a rule of life that everything you always wanted
Comes the very second you stop looking for it.

– Carrie Bradshaw, *Sex and the City*

Our wisdom comes from our experiences
And our experiences comes from our mistakes.

A friend is someone who knows your not perfect
But treats you as if you are.

A good friend is like a lightning bug
They light up your life when you need it the most
And least expect it.

– Friends light the way

While we have time
Lets do good.

– St. Frances of Assisi

In life we always look at the mountains ahead of us
and feel defeated.
We forget about the mountains we have
already climbed and survived.

– C.J. Marie

◆

The worst thing about being strong
Is that nobody knows when you are hurting.

◆

Memories remind us that nothing is forever
Time is precious and should not be wasted.
Enjoy life and remember don't count the days
Make the days count.

◆

You learn more from your losses
Than that of your wins.

– C.J. Marie

◆

You can't go in the future
If your past is present.

— Carrie Bradshaw, *Sex and the City*

No matter how far you go
There is no place far enough
to escape your past.

— Carrie Bradshaw, *Sex and the City*

Its great to be 70
But sometimes its just fun
to act like a 17 year old.

— C.J. Marie

A woman over 70 is not only sensational,
she has a super power called knowledge.

— C.J. Marie

Strut your wisdom like a peacock

You have earned it
You're a trailblazer.

– C.J. Marie

You are special in your
own extraordinary way.

– C.J. Marie

Fill your life with wonder
And the rest will be magical.

– C.J. Marie

In the second act of your life
Make it your best
Its your last chance.

– C.J. Marie

Time waits for no one
And there are no promises
of tomorrow.

– C. J. Marie

12 Things to Always Remember

1. *The past cannot be changed.*
2. *Opinions do not define your reality.*
3. *Everyone's journey is different.*
4. *Things always get better with time.*
5. *Judgements are a confession of character.*
6. *Overthinking leads us to sadness.*
7. *Happiness is found within.*
8. *Positive thoughts create positive outcomes.*
9. *Smiles are contagious.*
10. *Kindness is free.*
11. *You only fail if you quit.*
12. *What goes around comes around.*

– DEMIC

Time has passed and memories remain sacredly
In my heart. I am grateful for the time we spend together.
We talk, we laugh, and we remember days of long ago.
Thank you mom for bringing a smile to my face
and warmth to my heart

— C.J. Marie

Great things are done
By a series of small things
brought together.

— Vincent Van Gogh

This is the beginning of a new day.
You have been given this day to use
As you will. You can waste it or use it for good.
What you do today is important because you are exchanging
A day of your life for it. When tomorrow comes, this day will
be gone forever. In its place will be something you left behind.
Let it be something good.

Extraordinary times calls for extraordinary measures.

Strong women are not born
They are made by walking
Through the storms of life.

Live your unique self fearlessly.

— C.J. Marie

Embrace courage in the face of fear.

I love how summer just wraps
Its arms around you like
A warm blanket.

— Kellie Elmore

Those memories of you will always bring a smile
if only I could have you back for just a little while.
Then we could sit and talk again just like we used to do
You always meant so very much and always will too.
The fact that your no longer here will always cause me
Pain but your forever in my heart until we meet again.

◆

Never let fear stand in the way of your dreams.

◆

'Tis better to have loved and lost
than never have loved at all.

— Alfred Lord Tennyson

◆

Failure is a stepping stone to success.
There are only lessons learned and wisdom gained.

— C.J. Marie

◆

The difference between ordinary and extraordinary
Is that little extra.

◆

Perserverance towards any goal always wins.

– C.J. Marie

◆

Dance like nobody is watching, love like you've
Never been hurt. Sing like nobody's listening,
Live like it's heaven on earth.

– Mark Twain

◆

Sprinkle a little sunshine on someone's lonely life.

– C.J. Marie

◆

Having someplace to go to is home.
Having someone to love is family.
Having both is a blessing.

◆

Cherish the times spent
with family and loved ones.
Those are the greatest memories
you will ever make.

The key to aging is not to mourn what is lost
But to celebrate what remains.

— Mark Middleton

All that I am is because of you.
Who would I be if I had never been
loved by you?

— Michaela Angemeer

Own your dreams.
There is no better way to make them happen.

— Seth Godin

We are the dreamers of dreams.

– Roald Dahl

This day is a journey,
this very moment is an adventure.

– Rebecca Pavlenko

Sitting beneath a weeping willow tree embracing the shade
and solitude that surrounds me beneath its leaves,
I sit under this tree that symbolizes my soul.
This is my sanctuary of peace where I can go for comfort
and tranquility and listen to the whispers of my heart.
I need to pause from the noise of this world
to find the strength and courage to face this life
with love and understanding,
hoping to find some way
to bring kindness in these difficult times
we call humanity.

– C.J. Marie

Play is the highest form of research.

— Albert Einstein

Dream Big.
Dream without limitations.
Dream as if you'll live forever.
Dream as if it's all that matters.
Dream as if anything is possible...
Because it is.

— Kristina Karlsson

Actions Make
Dreams Happen

Dreams are wonderful, but they only remain thoughts, if no action is taken. Everyone should take time to dream. Motivation begins with a thought and lends itself to a dream. How many of us really live out the wishes of our hearts?

If the thought is strong and motivation is high, the wheels of determination begin to turn and speed the hope to achieve it step by step.

Some people laugh at dreams, they think they are impossible to conquer, this is when crippling thinking begins. If you think you can't, you won't and your dream melts away. Thoughts are the figment of the imagination and imagining can bring about fulfillment of those dreams.

Pursuing a dream takes work, sacrifice and determination. I believe people feel it takes too much time and effort so they surrender to the thought that it can never happen, so why even try. This is the biggest mistake of all, it takes on the defeatist's attitude. How do you know if you don't give it a try? Why give up before you even get started? Succumbing to defeat before you take any steps to put your thoughts into motion is a big mistake. My belief has always been that if you want something bad enough you do what it takes to achieve it.

Getting started and taking the first step is the most challenging. Many times, we become overwhelmed, and we don't know where to start, and dreams fade away. It is so gratifying when steps of accomplishment lead to victory. There will always be mistakes made but success comes from knowledge gained through our failures.

In my own life I have had many failures, but my drive is so great to pursue my goal that failure never discourages me from pressing forward. Some of my ventures have been victorious, some were not, the most important thing is that I put forth the effort and tried realizing I did my best and that is important to me.

Even if you can't reach the moon, landing on the stars is not so bad.

Dreams not only come true.
They can exceed your wildest expectations.

– Tiffany Loren Rowe

Dreaming after all,
is a form of planning.

– Gloria Steinem

Don't dream your life away.
Put action in your dream,
and just make it happen.

– C.J. Marie

Live in the sunshine,
swim in the sea,
drink the wild air.

– Ralph Waldo Emerson

Say yes to possibilities,
even if you think you can't.
More than likely you can.
Possibilities are opportunities
eager to be challenged.

–C.J. Marie

Goals are just dreams with deadlines.
Never look at failure as defeat,
it's one step closer to success.

– C.J. Marie

As long as your breathing
it's never too late.

– C.J. Marie

Shoot for the moon.
Even if you miss,
you'll land amoung the stars.

– Les Brown

A happy heart makes the face cheerful.

– Proverbs 15:13

Fear holds us back and keeps us from facing challenges..
Overcoming fear opens the door to opportunities.

– C. J. Marie

Worry is like a rocking chair.
It gives you something to do,
but it doesn't get you anywhere.

– Glenn Turner

The art of being wise
is the art of knowing
what to overlook.

– William James

Just learn to enjoy the journey of life.

Life is too short
to leave the key
to my happiness
in someone else's pocket.

We all have magic in our hearts
and goals in our souls.

There are moments that mark your life
and little things quite often
make a permanent home
in our memories.

Never a failure always a lesson.

– Rihanna

There will always be thorny patches
in life that allow us to appreciate
all the smooth ones.

– C.J. Marie

With every decade we live,
there is a transition.

– C.J. Marie

Be the Best at any Age
The 60s are Sexy
The 70s are Sensational
The 80s are Eccentric
The 90s are Notorious
The 100s are Historic

— C.J. Marie

Let your spirit soar.
Get swept away.
Feel nostalgic.
Sometimes I go
Boho style.

— C.J. Marie

Wishes without action
are only daydreams.

— C.J. Marie

I want to be an inspiration to others
showing that by determination,
unshakable principles, and endless enthusiasm
you can accomplish anything.

– C.J. Marie

There should be observation
without judgement.

– C.J. Marie

Your face reflects the feelings in your heart.

– C.J. Marie

Negative thoughts
will never give you a
positive life.

–Frank Bonsangue

The silver moon shining against a sapphire sky
hovering over the amber lights of the city.
The exquisite glow of lights awakens my heart
and transports me to a magical place
of warmth and tranquility.
I marvel at the beauty my eyes are beholding.
Night so warm and lights so bright,
a moon so white preparing for the light of day
bringing hope and a new beginning
of a better tomorrow.

– C.J. Marie

◆

When opportunity knocks,
open the door.
You never know where
it might lead.

◆

The greatest wealth is to live
content with very little.

– Plato

◆

Living Content

What I have found during the decades of my life is that you can't appreciate wealth if you always have it. Wealth can be defined in many ways. In the literal sense it is associated with money. Wealth can also be thought of in relation to having good health. Plato reveals a great deal in his simple quote. It can be interpreted in a variety of ways. When I see people in wheelchairs suffering from chronic illness or children suffering in hospitals, or the homeless living on the streets and subways, I have great appreciation and gratitude for the life I am living today.

I can walk, run, talk, think, and have a healthy family. Being mindful of what life is for others allows us to realize how blessed we are in our own lives. Plato had it right in his simple quote: "When you live with little you appreciate much more."

Becoming "spoiled" is a consequence of having too much of a good thing. Never forget where you came from and always help those in need. Superficial people rely on material things to boost their egos and appear affluent to others. It is important to them to make a statement to the world. It may be fun, but it is not the most important thing in life. Wise people are aware of this and they know that in a flash it could be taken away. Live joyfully with gratitude for all your blessings.

Winter reminds us that everyone
and everything needs some
quiet time.

— Katrina Meyer

Be the heroine in your life,
not the victim.

— Nora Ephron

The earth has its music
for those who listen.

—William Shakespeare

Stories are landscapes
of human experience.

Together we will build
a life we love.

— C.J. Marie

◆

Choose to live in the light,
Not in the darkness.

— C.J. Marie

◆

When we are raising our children
the days seem so long,
but the years pass so quickly.

— C.J. Marie

◆

Your smile is your logo
Your personality is your business card
How you leave others feeling after
Having an experience with you
Becomes your trademark.

— Jay Danzie

◆

A Bond Like No Other

So many thoughts go through my mind as I look into my little baby boy's face. The love I feel is profound, sacred and a joy beyond words. It is the love between a mother and her son. It is love like no other. As I held my baby boy, I knew in my heart that he would mean everything to me and I would be his world too, even if it is for a very short time.

I will hold his hand and calm his fears and share in all his joys and excitement as I guide him through life. It is me he looks for to make his world right when it goes wrong. I solve his problems and comfort him like no one else could. He cries when I leave and wants to always be with me. I am his first love, and we love our time together.

Life goes on and my little boy grows up. He is not my little boy anymore and there is someone else to take my place. She is all that I was to him. He looks to her the same way he once looked at me. As painful and empty as it is I would not have it any other way.

Life passes, and we age, and I have returned to my second childhood. Now it is me who needs my little boy to hold my hand

and help me do things that once were simple. Please help me walk and comfort my fears when I feel lost and confused. Help me make my world right when I don't know where I'm going or what I'm doing. Time does this to so many.

We go away from being the person we once were. Please be patient with me, wipe away my tears and fears. As you look into my eyes remember our special "together times" we shared. Now I need you. I am alone and I can't remember much, but one thing I will never forget is how much I love you and that bond will never be broken. Be with me, stay with me, even if it's just for a very short time.

Someday when the pages of my life end,
I know that you will be one of the beautiful chapters.
Always keep me in your heart
as you are always in my mine.
Nothing and nobody will ever change it.

◆

We are the artist of our own life's canvas.
The colors are vibrant, yet muttered.
Life can be vibrant, wild painful, and exciting.
Nothing and nobody is perfect.

◆

Life is like an echo
What you send out comes back
What you sow you reap.
What you give you get.
What you see in others exists in you.

– Zig Ziglar

*If it's out of your hands
it deserves freedom.*

*Life is not about who you once were,
It's about who you are now,
and who you have the potential to be.*

*You can be gorgeous at thirty,
charming at forty and
irresistible for the rest of your life.*

— CoCo Chanel

*Nothing will work
Unless you do.*

— Maya Angelou

Aging is years of wisdom yearning to be shared.

— C.J. Marie

Just watching your days drift by
means nothing unless you make
them meaningful.

— C.J. Marie

Every problem we face in life
teaches us something if we
we are open to learn.

— C.J. Marie

Good could come out of every situation
if you have the wisdom to see it.

— C.J. Marie

Being happy doesn't mean life is perfect.
It means you decided to
look beyond perfection.

— Brightside.me

Children are the rainbows of life.
Grandchildren are the pot of gold.

In the blink of an eye everything can change.
So forgive often and love with all your heart.
You never know when you may have the chance again.

— I believe.com

There is no substitute for victory.

Memories are forged in the sand
and photos document these memories
to hang on the wall.

When you can tell your story
and it doesn't make you cry,
you know you have healed.

As I listen to songs from many years ago
I realize how far away I am from the hopes
and dreams I had back then.

◆

What years take away is given back
with wisdom, insight and knowledge.

◆

Winning is when preparation
meets opportunity.

◆

Life without risk
is no life at all.
Live life without limits.

– Demi Moore as Diana Murphy in *Indecent Proposal*

Where Have All Our Values Gone?

Respect, responsibility, accountability, loyalty, knowledge, inspiration, recognition, and family. Where have they all gone? As I observe the attitude of our young people today, I question; how they came to develop their ideas about life. Call it age, or just the way the direction of the world is going, it is all foreign in comparison to the world we once knew.

What happened to accountability for the decisions people in our society make? How did people get to not care and become so self-centered? Where did the sense of conscience go? Kindness towards one another has faded away, replaced by anger, violence, and hate. Where are we headed? Youth seems to have entitlement as their name of the game. Government handouts are a way of life for many. People would rather stay home instead of working. Self-pride has diminished. Challenging work and grit in order to reach success are gone.

The world we live in today compared to years ago has become unrecognizable. I am concerned about our young people who are confronted with this new world of ideas and transitions. This generation knowns no difference, they have nothing to compare it to.

As a woman of age, I am grateful to never have been faced with generational turmoil. As the world keeps turning this too will pass, but the reality is it will never return to the carefree days we once knew long ago.

Experience is priceless.
It's a shame you have to pay for
it with your youth.

— Steve Harvey

◆

Rise from the flames of anger.
Forgive and move on.

—C.J. Marie

◆

No day shall erase you
from the memory of time.

— Virgil

◆

Live your life instead of obsessing about it.

— C.J. Marie

◆

Freedom comes from letting go
of people and things that give you pain.
Only then can we live a life worthy of living in this world.

– C.J. Marie

The difference between a vision and a mission is,
a mission is the way we make a vission happen.

– C.J. Marie

Live out loud,
be heard, be proud
and know you are important.

–C.J. Marie

Memories are our life's treasures.

– C.J. Marie

Winners never set limits
They always set goals.

◆

Where there's smoke there's fire.

◆

Don't be quick to believe what you hear,
because lies spread faster than truth.

◆

Life's tragedy is that we get old too soon
and wise too late.

— Benjamin Franklin

◆

"The heart has its reasons
which reason knows nothing of...
We know the truth not only by the reason,
but by the heart."

— Blaise Pascal, *Pensées*

◆

I'd rather regret the things I've done

than regret the things I haven't done.

— Lucille Ball

Vintage is aged to perfection.

How can a true mother cut a child out of her life?
I thought a mother's love was unconditional.

— C.J. Marie

We have defied the odds
And have shattered expectations.
The best ideas come from solving problems.

I lost myself trying to please everyone
Now I'm losing everyone as I find myself.

If you believe you can, you will.
If you don't, you won't.

◆

Learn to embrace your imperfections.
It's those unique differences
that make you extraordinary.

◆

Celebrate you age many never make it.

◆

Listen and silent have the same letters.
Remember to be silent and listen carefully.

◆

You have to be unique and different
and shine in your own way.

— Lady Gaga

◆

I do what I please
and I do it with ease.

— Martha Stewart

Behind every strong woman
lies a broken little girl
who learned how to get back up
and depend on herself.

The worst thing in life isn't being lonely,
it's being forgotten.

Challenge makes champions.

You never fail unless you give up.

Take tradition and decorate it your way.

Don't use fear of other's negative opinions
as an excuse to not move ahead.
Don't let people into your vision if
they don't match your intention.

– F.L. Richards

Youth is wasted on the young.

– Bernard Shaw

Be the very best version of yourself.

– C.J. Marie

Strength comes from struggle.

The sad part of getting older is that
no one can see you're still young inside.

◆

Women of wisdom are driven by purpose.

◆

Never regret a day in your life.
Good days give happiness,
bad days give experience,
worst days give lessons,
and the best days give memories.

◆

You can never go back to the way life used to be...
Time moves on.

— C.J. Marie

◆

Never be a prisoner of your past.
It was just a lesson not a life sentence.

◆

*The difference between winning
and losing is detail.*

◆

*Attitude is ageless.
It's like an injection of youth.*

◆

We are little fish in a big pond.

◆

*Man lives once as a man
and twice as a child.*

◆

*Worry doesn't take away tomorrow's troubles,
it takes away todays peace.*

◆

There is a bit of heaven in every friendship.

◆

"Well done is better than well said. "

— Benjamin Franklin

Every action gets a reaction.

*The biggest mistake we make in life
is thinking that we have time.*

— Buddha

What good is wisdom if we can't share it with others.

*Memories are treasures of the heart
always to be remembered.*

— C.J. Marie

Live by the sun.
Dream by the moon.
Wish by the stars.

◆

Life has more imagination than
we carry in our dreams.

◆

Nothing is ever lost if you follow your heart.

◆

I am not apologizing for being me.

◆

It's easier to beg for forgiveness
Than to ask for permission.

– Rear Admiral Grace Hopper

◆

Strong people forgive,
intelligent people ignore.

There are lessons to be learned and wisdom to be gained
when you listen to someones's pain.

– C.J. Marie

The beauty in life is can easily be seen
when you take the time
to open your eyes.

– C.J. Marie

Make your years count,
don't count the years.

You can't get to the future
if your past is present.

*It's simple to
go the extra mile and
you will stand out in a crowd.*

– Robin Crow

*Our wisdom comes from experiences
and our experience comes from our mistakes.*

*If you are comfortable in your own skin
and you're comfortable in your own life,
you will totally live life your way.*

*A friend is someone who knows you're not perfect
but treats you as if you were.*

While we have time, let us do good.

— St. Frances of Assisi

When we get to the end of our lives together
the house we had,
the cars we drove,
the things we possessed won't matter.
What will matter is that
I had you and you had me.

— Wonder Point décor

Don't let someone dim your light
simply because it's shining in their eyes.

— Facebook - I Walk in My Shoes

Strut your wisdom like a peacock.
You are a trailblazer.

— C.J. Marie

You are special
in your own unique and
extraordinary way.

– C.J. Marie

Love who you are.
There is no one like you in the world.

– C.J. Marie

People who are hurt,
hurt others.

We should lift each other up
and cheer each other on,
not try to outshine one another.
The sky would be awfully dark
with just one star.

– Stacie

Don't allow people to make you feel
bad or guilty for living your life.
It is your life —
live it the way you want.

— Lessons Taught By Life

Keep going. You got this.

— Life Quotes

Don't you dare let people tell you
you're too old or that it's too late.
If you're still standing, then anything is possible.
Own your awesomeness and show everyone that
greatness doesn't have an experation date.
The only reason people hold onto memories
so tightly is because memories are the only things
that don't change when everything else does.

Words without effort is meaningless.

Christmas wishes and mistletoe kisses.

Champagne wishes and cavier dreams.

Love doesn't need to be perfect
It just needs to be true.

– Thoughts Wonder

I am in competition with no one.
I have no desire to play the game
of being better than anyone.
I'm simply trying to be a better person
than I was yesterday.

– Positive Corners

There Will Never Be Another You

There is only one you. There are no duplicates or copies. You are unique and special in your own way. Sometimes we go through life wanting to be someone else. We compare ourselves to others in every way, The question we ask ourselves on an unconscious level is, are we good enough? Am I too short, too fat, too skinny, and the list goes on.

It is important to embrace self-acceptance. We need to put our flaws in check and not allow them to be amplified in our minds. Society leads us down the path of unworthiness, then the media and print forces us to look at our flaws through a different lens. Perfection does not exist. Embrace who you are and be the best version of yourself.

We are all imperfections and a work in progress. No one will ever be perfect. We are all special in our own "unique" way.

Life is so ironic. It takes sadness to know happiness,
Noise to appreciate silence, and absence to value presence.

– The Wise You

To take care of those who once took care of us
Is one of the highest honors in life.

– The Walker

At the end of the day
what really matters is that you loved well.
You've done your best and you're thankful
for all that you have.

– Insta Quotes

Remember, we don't control what happens,
we control how we respond to it.

–Via, *Dark Secrets*

*Stay true to yourself
and never let anyone
dim your lights.*

– Goalcast

*Enjoy life!
You never know
how much time you have left.*

– Lessons Learned In Life Inc.

*Once you've matured,
you will realize that silence
is more important than proving a point.*

– Lessons Taught By Life

*I don't know how to act my age
I have never been this age before.*

– Hilarious Texts

*Never laugh at someone's situation
because you just never know if
someday you will find yourself in
the very same position.*

– Live to Inspire

*Always keep in mind
haters spread rumors,
fools spread them,
and idiots believe them.*

– Lessons taught By Life

*The older I get,
the less I care about what people think of me.
Therefore, the older I get
the more I enjoy life.*

– Lessons Learned In Life Inc.

◆

Never forget how far you've come.
Everything you have gotten through,
all the times you have pushed on
even when you felt you couldn't,
all the mornings you got out of bed
no matter how hard it was,
all the times you wanted to give up
but you got through another day.
Never forget how much strength you
have learned and developed along the way.

−Lessons Taught By Life

Its not about perfect.
It's about effort,
and when you bring that effort every single day,
that's when the transformation happens.

− Jillian Michaels

You know who you are. You know your true colors.
Don't let anyone paint you differently.

— Lessons Learned In Life Inc.

One day you are going to hug your last hug,
kiss your last kiss and hear someone's voice for the last time.
But you never know when the last time will be,
so live every day as if it were the last time
you will be with the person you love.

—DEMIC

Don't let bitter, angry people drag you down to their level.
Instead, use their behavior as an example
of how not to behave
and be grateful you are nothing like them.

— The Wise You

Failures are part of life.
If you don't fail, you don't learn.
If you don't learn, you'll never change.

– DEMIC

On this road called life
you have to take the good with the bad,
Smile with the sad, love what you have,
and remember what you had.
Always forgive, learn from your mistakes
but never forget.
People change, things go wrong,
but just remember the ride still goes on.

– Lessons learned in Life Inc.

I really saw clearly, and for the first time,
why a mother is really important...
she stands between the unknown and the known.

– Maya Angelou

Purpose

I am sure, like me, you have stopped and thought about what your purpose is in life. So many of us go through life just day to day. Working hard, raising children, paying bills and if you're lucky taking a well-deserved vacation. There is more to life than just routines.

Do you stop and think about all that you do without resentment and wonder towards those who were born financially wealthy? Even those who are affluent in our society have their problems too. Many resent those who live their life in a luxurious way. It is clear we all have a purpose in life. Many of us never figure out what our purpose is. Your insightfulness and mindfulness determine your purpose. Everyone serves their purpose every day by what they do in life. Whatever you choose to do in life is your purpose.

What is Mindfulness? It is being aware, taking notice, living in the moment, and feeling it. Most people are not open-minded to this. They go through life waiting for life to happen. Years drift by and they realize they never really lived. They merely existed, doing what was required of them. This is a sad commentary for some people. Granted life is not easy and it is not always the happiest either, but you can find peace in it if you are mindful. Live in the moment, observe it, feel the feeling, and enjoy what gives you pleasure. Be aware of your feelings of joy and content.

I have found that most people rush through life with a negative frame of mind. They are angry with life. In this difficult world we live in we must take the time to internalize the good times and feel the joy because if you don't, they will be gone forever.

Be the best kind of beautiful.

– C.J. Marie

The only things you can take with you
when you leave this world
are the things you've packed inside your heart.

– Susan Gale

Time is like a river –
you can't touch the same water twice,
because the flow that has passed
will never pass again.
Enjoy every moment of your life.

– Lessons Taught By Life

Dance before the music stops.
Live before life is over.

– Live to Inspire

It's your road and yours alone.
Others may walk with you,
but no one can walk it for you.

— The Wise You

Wisdom learned is wisdom gained.
Wisdom inspires attitude.

— C.J. Marie

Before you judge my life, my past, or my character,
walk in my shoes, walk the path I have traveled,
live my sorrow, my doubts, my fears, my pain,
and my laughter.
Remember: "Judge not lest ye be judged."
Everyone has their own story.
When you have lived my life, then you can judge me.

— Million feelings
Poster based in the United Kingdom, Sept.26, 2016

Don't aim to be liked,
aim to be real.
You will get a lot of respect.

– Live to Inspire

Dream big.
Start small
But most of all start.

– Simon Sinek

If you don't separate yourself from your distractions,
your distractions will eventually separate you from
your goals and the life you want.

◆

Everyone is a perfect imperfection —
a work in progress.
We are all trying to be extraordinary
in our own unique way.

– C.J. Marie

◆

I usually give people more chances than they deserve,
but once I'm done, I'm done.

– Lessons Learned In Life

Live your life to the fullest.
It's the only one you've got.

– C.J. Marie

When our time on this earth is done.
Money and material things will not matter
but the love, time, and kindness we've given others
will shine and live on forever.

Life is filled with challenges.
Don't let happiness be one of them.
Be Happy.

– Thoughts Wonder

Don't compare yourself with others
No one can play your role
Better than you.

— Thoughts Wonder

A Dreamer

Harriet Tubman said, "Every Great Dream Begins with a Dreamer." How many of us really have a dream? Most people let life unfold. They go with the flow with the fear of making the wrong decisions. A dream is just a dream unless there is motion behind it. When a person fulfills a dream, the feeling is extraordinary.

Dreamers must be doers to achieve their highest potential. What stops a person from pursuing their dream? Is it fear? Is it overwhelming? Or is it just too much work? Maybe it's just not important enough. People have multiple excuses for not going after what they truly want in life. Life is built on hopes and dreams. If we don't try, then what is life about?

Live in the warmth of the sun.
Cleanse your soul in the sea.
Breath in the salted air.
Let your toes wiggle in the sand.
Thank you for this beautiful world.

– C.J. Marie

Without boundaries we all go further.

The greatest happiness in the world
is to make others happy.

– Luther Burbank

Good things come to those who wait.
Better things come to those who don't give up
and the best things come to those who believe.

As we grow older,
real beauty travels from the face to the heart.
Appeal turns to charm,
hurt to wisdom and great moments to shared memories.
The true beauty in life is not how happy you are now,
but how happy others are because of you.

Life is an extraordinary venture
filled with ordinary happenings.

– C.J. Marie

Love endures all things.

When you truly love someone,
love brilliantly.

– C. J. Marie

They say I changed a lot.
I said a lot has changed me.

– Lessons Learned in Life Inc.

There is something about relationships...
Sometimes they look perfect on the outside
but are very different on the inside.

– C.J. Marie

Love always challenges endurance.

– C.J. Marie

Sometimes its easy to forgive the mistakes of others
but it's hard to rebuild the trust that has been destroyed.

– The Wise You

The one who falls and gets up
is stronger than the one who never fell.

– Thoughts Wonder

Don't waste your words on people who deserve your silence.
Sometimes the most powerful thing you can say
is nothing at all.

– Mandy Hale

Some of the most beautiful things in your life
come unexpectedly.
Believe

– Thoughts Wonder

It's better to walk alone
than to walk with a crowd going in the wrong direction.

– Herman SU

Let your smile change the world.
Don't let the world change your smile.

– Thoughts Wonder

Its never too late for a new beginning in your life.

– Thoughts Wonder

The tongue has no bones
but it's strong enough to break a heart.
So be careful with your words.

– Harold Vaughan

One of the happiest moments in life
is when you find the courage to let go
of what you can't change.

– Lessons Learned In Life Inc.

Do good.
It will come back to you in unexpected ways.

— Thoughts Wonder

Life is not fair, it never was,
it isn't now and it won't ever be.
Do not fall into the trap.
The entitlement trap of feeling like a victm.

— Matthew Mc Conaughey

No matter how kind or generous you are,
you will never satisfy
an ungrateful person.

— DEMIC

There is no need to drive me crazy.
I'm close enough to walk.

Only people who aren't happy with themselves
are mean to others.
Remember that.

– Thoughts Wonder

It's Never too Late

If you think it's too late, then it is. You make up your mind, you feel if you try you are not going to get it. You couldn't be more wrong in thinking and having this negative attitude. If it's important for you to go forward, there is nothing in life that is a waste of time.

When thoughts like this saturate your mind ask yourself this question "How much do I really want to achieve this dream?" Whatever your decision is reveals how important this goal is to you. Pursue the dream, take on the challenge. You never know what you can accomplish if you don't give it your best.

Not everyone will have the heart you have.
Not everyone will appreciate you and what you do for them.
Sometimes it won't be easy having a kind heart
in a cruel world. Be prepared.

— Tony Gaskins Jr.

◆

The moment you feel
you have to prove your worth to someone
is the moment to absolutely and utterly walk away.

— Alysia Harris

◆

Some will get great pleasure
in provoking a reaction from you.
That's when you need to discover the
great pleasure of giving them none.

— JM Storm

◆

Richest wealth is Wisdom
Strongest weapon is Patience
Best security is Faith
Most effective tonic is
Laughter and Surprisingly all are free.

– DEMIC

"The world is so unpredictable.
Things happen suddenly, unexpectedly.
We want to feel we are in control of our own existence.
In some ways we are, in some ways we are not.
We are ruled by the forces of chance and coincidence."

– Paul Auster

My Broken World

When did the world become so broken? When did hate and violence take on our world?

When did respect for life and kindness towards one another become obsolete? Our world has become a dangerous place. Who can you trust anymore? Where has our humanity gone? Why are we so defensive and divided?

Every word we say today in conversation must be carefully selected so as not to offend anyone. Despite the evil that surrounds us I go with peace, shutting out the toxic noise of those who interfere with peace of mind. They will not turn me into who they want me to be and believe in their destructive ways. Their beliefs are breaking down our beautiful world killing life and love.

I turn off the chaos, the lies, the propaganda of everyone wanting to prove their point of being right. I live my life to be kind and good and I won't give in to anyone. No one should define who you are, and you should stand up for what you believe in even if you must stand alone.

Stand up for what you believe in,
even if your left standing alone.

– C.J. Marie

Be a girl with a mind.
A woman with attitude.
And a lady with class.

– Quote Remedy

Loyalty is hard to find.
Trust is easy to loose.
Actions speak louder than words.

– Thoughts Wonder

Two things define us:
our patience when we have nothing
and our attitude when we have everything.

– Quote Remedy

Sometimes the hardest fight
is against yourself.

– The Wise You

◆

Push yourself
because no one is going to do it for you.

– Thoughts Wonder

◆

A strong woman
will always turn her pain into power.

– The Ravenwolf

◆

When something bad happens,
you have these choices:
you can either let it define you,
let it destroy you,
or you can let it strengthen you.

– Dr. Seuss

◆

Be happy for this moment.
This moment is your life.

– Thoughts Wonder

Choose a good heart not a good face.

– DEMIC

You are very powerful
provided you know how powerful you are.

– Yogi Bhajan

Life has taught me that you can't control someones loyalty.
No matter how good you are to them, doesn't mean they'll
treat you the same. No matter how much they mean to you
doesn't mean they'll value you the same. Sometimes the peo-
ple you love the most, turn out to be the people
You can trust the least.

– Trent Shelton

The important part is that you are trying,
you will figure it out.
Just be patient and be commited to the path.

– Thoughts Wonder

Don't wait for things to get easier, simpler, or better.
Life will always be complicated,
learn to be happy right now.
Otherwise you'll run out of time.

– Live To Inspire

I have come to realize that the only people
I need in my life are the ones who need me in theirs,
even when I have nothing else to
offer them but myself.

I may not be everyones cup of tea,
but I am someones double shot of tequila.

♦

*Sometimes miracles are just
people with kind hearts.*

– Thoughts Wonder

*She was like a beautiful flower,
but age had her wilting away day by day.*

– C.J. Marie

♦

*You don't have forever to live,
where you go whatever you do,
strive to leave footprints of love,
kindness and peace.
Make the world glad you lived.*

– Mordy quotes

An Alzheimer's - Dementia Poem

Don't ask me to remember,
Don't ask me to understand,
Let me rest and know you are with me.
Kiss my cheek and hold my hand.
I'm confused beyond your concept.
I am sad, sick and lost.
All I know is that I need you to be with me at all cost.
Don't lose your patience with me,
don't scold me, curse or cry.
I can't help the way I'm acting.
I can't be different though I try.
Just remember that I need you that the best of me is gone.
Please don't fail to stand beside me,
Love me till my life is gone.

◆

Memories
to Carry Me Forever

As I read the poem on the previous page, thoughts of my mother filled my heart. These words are true from a person suffering from Alzheimer's or Dementia. I remember when I would sit with my mom, she would say to me, "I'm going away."

I would hold her hand and say, "I am here now and that's what is important." She would squeeze my hand and smile and touch my cheek.

I remember those days when we would sit and talk and just spend time together reminiscing about days long ago. It was amazing how clearly she remembered those days and forgot what she had done five minutes ago. It is such a dreadful disease.

I will never forget the look on her face when it was time for me to leave. I always left her with a heavy heart. I visited my mother almost every day and spent a great deal of time with her until the pandemic hit. It was very difficult for me not being able to go and be with her during that time. I am grateful that she never got COVID, and after a period of time I was able to visit her again.

The memories I made with her in the nursing home will carry with me forever. She would say, "I don't have much to go. I will be leaving you soon."

I would respond and say, "Wait for me and meet me at heaven's door with Nona and Nonno (my grandparents)." She would laugh and we would laugh together. I told her, "Don't worry, Mom, we will all be together again."

She said with a melancholy look in her eye, "I hope so."

This poem was very emotional for me because it brought back memories of my mother. I am grateful beyond words that I spent those days with her. I will treasure them always. She was like a beautiful flower, wilting away, day by day. The takeaway is live in the moment, and always have the special people in your life know how much they are loved.

Essay Titles of Reflections

Stay connected to yourself and remember the bond you have with yourself, is a **BOND LIKE NO OTHER.** Do not get caught up in the web of **FLASHBACKS** from the past. Instead, **LIVE IN THE MOMENT. EVERY GREAT DREAM BEGINS WITH A DREAMER** and **ACTIONS MAKE DREAMS HAPPEN.** We all have a **PURPOSE** to be an inspiration to others in **MY BROKEN WORLD** of **POSSIBILITIES.** Children are our jewels of life and our hope for tomorrow. They are the memories we carry with us forever. As I have observed them…" As I have observed them, I question, **WHERE HAVE OUR VALUES GONE?** Their idea of entitlement has shadowed what Plato said, "The greatest gift is to live content with little" so live with gratitude for all the blessings you do have.

Final Thoughts

As I compiled this collection of writings the one thing that stood out in my mind was the importance of hope. Without hope in our lives, we have nothing. We must believe in ourselves and keep hope in our hearts as we live our lives day after day. It all begins with a simple thought and the feelings behind that thought. Life is what you make it, so make it your best.

The opposite of hope is despair and to live life to its fullest hope must be the catalyst that is the driving factor in each of us to be our best self. With hope, we press forward to make this world a better place to live our Best Life.

.

www.ingramcontent.com/pod-product-compliance
Lightning Source LLC
Chambersburg PA
CBHW021649120626
46545CB00002B/765